TITANIA'S WISHING SPELLS

LOVE

TITANIA HARDIE

QUADRILLE

FOR SAMANTHA AND ZEPHYRINE

The subject of love, and questions pertaining to it, seems to go hand in hand with the idea of magic. Attractions occur without rhyme or reason, meetings are so often by the merest thread of chance, and our psychological state runs hot and cold in the business of falling in love, and in maintaining intense interest.

In days past, a young girl's only chance of respectability was marriage, so the need for finding a marriage partner was as serious a concern for a milk-maid as it was for one of Jane Austen's heroines. Then, too, finding someone who would tie the knot was no guarantee of joy. Rather delightfully, a thousand ways of influencing the odds for happiness or trying to understand Fate's workings grew up, mostly around the old wise woman's lore of herbal spells and divination.

In this little book you will find a selection of old, tried-and-true spells for enhancing an existing love relationship, or enticing a reticent lover into closer confidence with the spell-maker, or mending a broken heart, or indeed, finding out whether the one you want is the right one for you. My belief is that we make them work through our own concentrated belief: spells focus the mind, which is capable of miraculous actions.

I wish you joy and success, as well as much fun, in the pages ahead.

Diamonds

These precious love stones are a natural choice for lovers who have decided to make their commitment, and it would be churlish not to see a gift of a diamond as a true token of deep love. This, though, is a spell using a diamond both to test the strength of a suitor's attentions, and to strengthen the love itself.

Hold a diamond in your hand and close your fist, thinking of the face of your lover or the person you like so much, as you do so.

Ask the Lady of the Stone to reveal the depth of his or her attachment to you, and to show you how to make the bond stronger if need be; then place the diamond under your pillow, wrapped in soft cloth so that it won't get lost.

You will dream a clear dream of love if the relationship is already growing nicely; and you will be given a straightforward vision of what to do to improve things and charm the other party into deeper affection.

Make sure to carry the diamond – now a part of your love tie – with you to the next meeting you have with your loved one.

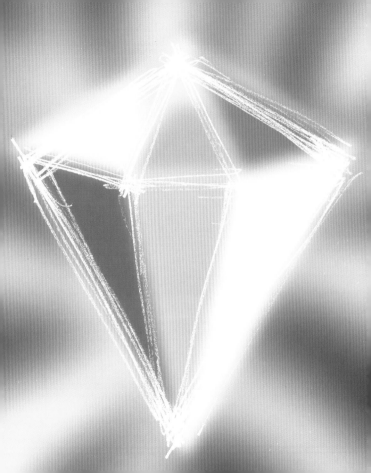

BRIDAL PINS

If a friend is about to be married and you are still looking for someone in your love life, ask the bride to give you two of the pins from the fitting of her dress.

"Wish upon a pin for joy; Soon you'll meet your special boy!" Hold the pins to your heart and wish very hard for a lover of your own.

Tuck one of the pins into your bodice or jacket, and cast the other into a fire saying: "May my heart soon be aflame with love".

Keep the pin you are wearing, and transfer it from outfit to outfit until the wedding takes place: most importantly, wear it on the day itself.

Kiss the bride who gave you the pins three times for luck after the ceremony, and you should be lucky enough to meet someone special before the moon has set that night.

Eggs

If you like someone very much, take care with your eggs.

If you bring your eggs home and break one getting it indoors, it is best to break another within the hour. Likewise, if you are baking and one breaks, try to contrive to break another, for the saying goes: "Break an egg, break a leg; break two, your love is true!"

Take some of the eggshell from the broken egg/s, and place them, together with the name of your loved one written on paper, in a blue dish. Cover them with a little water and let it stand overnight.

In the morning, plant the shells and paper in a pot with a blue plant, such as a hydrangea or hyacinth; water it in with the water.

Your love will now begin to grow true-blue, and your plant should thrive.

NB: If the egg you break is a double-yolker, marriage looks to be soon ahead.

SAGE LEAVES

At midnight on All Saints Day, Valentine's Day, or May Eve (the best):

Rush into the garden and pluck one sage leaf for every strike of the clock. (Have a pot on a balcony or windowsill if you live in a city).

Hold all twelve leaves in the palms of your hands, and wish for wisdom and rejoicing with the one you love.

Sleep on the leaves, which you should place reverently under your pillow. You will dream your success or failure with the object of your affection.

To keep the love growing, feed one of the sage leaves to your beloved in his or her food, but secretly!

Ivy leaf

Considered even more efficacious for persuading the gods to give you the love you desire than the sage leaves mentioned on the previous page.

Wish for the love of one special person as you pluck an ivy leaf unobserved in a quiet garden or woodland.

Place the leaf against your chest or bosom, and say: "Ivy, ivy, I love thee, In my bosom I place thee; And if the love I love calls me, Sure my own true love he (or she) must be, And happy we will be."

Place the leaf next to a picture, or possession, of the one you love, and your love should cling together more closely from now on. If your lover calls you, or visits, unexpectedly within a short time of doing this spell, you know it is the right love for you.

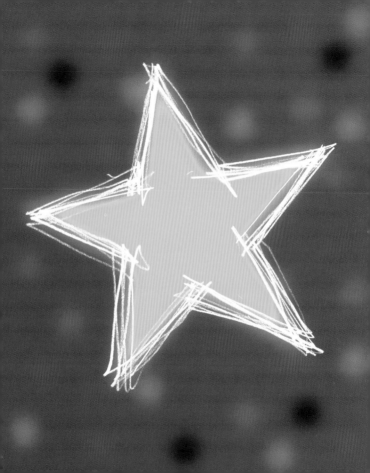

Myrtle

The famous talisman carried in Queen Victoria's
wedding bouquet. This wonderful, fragrant plant
is a special emissary for lovers.

If you have no love in your life, plant a myrtle on either side
of your door, and place a small five-pointed star at the base of
each plant. Love will soon enter your life, and peace and love
will together be attracted to your home.

If you want to gently strengthen someone's feelings for you,
or if the relationship has been growing too slowly, place a few
myrtle leaves in a cooked dish for him (or her) and ask the
goddess (for whom myrtle is sacred) to deepen his/her appetite
for you as well. Also, place a leaf of myrtle in your lover's
pocket "for luck". The tie will grow richer and sweeter.

Carry a sprig of myrtle in your wedding clothes, or bouquet;
the love will deepen with time.

Placed in a baby's cradle the baby will have a sunny, loving heart.

Hairpin

A lovely spell to do if your hairpin, or a comb in your hair, suddenly loosens.

A pin falling from your hair indicates that someone you love is thinking about you. Straight away take up the pin or comb and say your beloved's name three times over in a whisper. If you have not heard from the person for a little while and you want them now to get in touch, vividly imagine their face, and see yourself playing with his (or her) hair, caressing the temples and planting light kisses on your loved one's brow.

Replace the pin in your hair, and your love should suddenly be desperate to get in touch; you will certainly hear news before long.

MAY DEW

This precious moisture, collected on May morning and throughout the month, was valued for its cosmetic and health-giving powers, but it is especially useful for love spells.

Place a silver dish out overnight on May Eve (or any other night in the same month) and collect up all the dews on May morning. Place one drop of the liquid on your lips and say your love's name out loud.

Toss a few drops over your left shoulder and wish strongly for love to grow sweetly and happily between you.

Make up a love potion with some May flowers (pansies and early roses are usual) and a vanilla pod steeped in wine or champagne; add a few drops of the May dew at the end. Your love will grow bold and demonstrative in a way you have never witnessed before.

Knots #1

Knots could be cast, in days gone by, for good or ill. If a witch was cross she could knot a cord to hinder the conception or birth of a child; but if she was on side, she could hitch a knot that would secure a lover for an unattached girl or man.

If you are sleeping in a foreign place, or strange bed, take the chance to cast around for a love affair; or strengthen the bond you have with someone you've recently met, so your absence makes their heart grow fonder.

If your hair is long enough, tie the top into a knot, and if not, tie your undergarments once into a knot, saying: "This knot I knit, this knot I tie, To find my love, As he (she) goes by, In fine apparel and array, As he (she) may dress in every day." The knotted underwear was sometimes tied to a bed-post, but this is not essential if your bed has no posts.

During your sleep your love will appear before you, and the clothes he (she) wears will indicate his (her) profession. Books will show a scholar, paper reveal someone in law or accounting, and paints or a musical instrument reveal someone connected with arts, and so on.

If you have someone in mind, say their name as you make the knots, and your dream shall confide whether your affair will prosper.

Knots #2

This is the spell to use to make an existing relationship more steadfast, or even to nudge it towards the altar.

Cut a few strands of your hair and tie three knots in them; say your loved one's name over thrice as you do this.

Slip the knotted lock into your sweetheart's pocket or shoe, and for the next twenty-four hours say very little to your lover, or if it can be achieved without rudeness, nothing at all. Smile, rather, with your eyes to your lover's eyes.

Within a month the spell will strengthen the love-bond; but your wish for betrothal must be granted within a year, or it may never come at all.

BAY LEAVES

Trusted for generations as a love talisman for
Valentine's Day.

On the evening of the 13th, sprinkle rosewater on two bay
leaves and place them in a cross shape under your pillow.
Take four more and place one at each corner of your pillow:
six in total, the number of love.

Put on a clean T-shirt or nightdress, pure white in colour, and
sprinkle this too with rosewater. Now think hard of your lover's
face, and make the following pledge: "I will not be jealous but
will trust in you, and I will not be possessive but give time
and space to you; I will have confidence in your actions and
dealings, and I will chide gently if you hurt my feelings;
In short I will love you, and believe that you must love me
too, if here you will be".

During your dreams your love will answer you, and give you a
sign of fidelity on Valentine's Day. If you have no special love,
but do the regime above, you will soon find a partner.

CANDLES

A vital element in all magic-making, this spell for getting noticed by someone you like, or moving an existing romance on a peg is very powerful indeed. Make sure your thoughts and intentions are all honourable, and that you are not poaching someone else's partner.

Take a pin and stick it through a candle towards the top, but making sure it pierces the wick. As you do this, say: "Tis not only this candle I mean to stick, but .....'s heart too which I mean to prick; Whether he is now waking or sleeping, May he come to me that we soon shall be speaking."

Write your love's name on a piece of paper, and use this to light the candle, uttering his or her name as you do so.

If a ring appears to glow around the flame, you will have your wish before the moon expires; the ring itself often portends a wedding. If a spark flies from the flame, you will have a letter or phone call from your love within a day or so.

FOUR-LEAVED CLOVER

This is the symbol everyone wishes to find for a score of happy omens. In love:

If you are walking out to meet your love and you find a four-leaved clover on the way, your love will blossom and your lover prove true. Treasure it always.

If you are single but you come across a four-leaved clover by chance, pluck it and at once close your eyes, asking for the blessing of a happy heart. You will very shortly meet your true love, but again, must keep the clover safe.

If you want to find out how someone you like a lot feels about you, write his or her name on paper and seal it in an envelope with a four-leaved clover. Within four days or four weeks, you will have a declaration – one way or the other.

If you want simply to be lucky in love, touch the third leaf around from the top, going clockwise, this leaf is dedicated to love. Open your heart to light, luck and love, and your fortunes in romance will suddenly improve.

BRIDAL CAKE

When you next attend a wedding, choose this
from among a dozen practices if you would
soon be wed.

Quietly ask the bride to squeeze a small piece of the wedding
cake through her wedding ring, then take it home wrapped in
silk – not a paper napkin.

Write your name on a piece of paper, slip it into an envelope,
put in some rose petals (from the wedding if possible, otherwise
at least some which are fragrant), and add the silk-wrapped
cake. Place the envelope under your pillow.

You will dream of your love, but you must then keep the cake,
petals and envelope if you wish for a proposal. Dowse all in rose
perfume, and tie them together with a pink ribbon. Before the
year's date reappears, your wish will be granted.

Rainbow of love

A spell to make when you see a bright rainbow
in any place or at any time.

Touch the colours you see in the rainbow anywhere around you
– on your clothes, in your office, in your car, on flowers
growing in the garden – anywhere you can actually touch
anything that matches the colours of the rainbow.

As you touch each coloured item, say the following words, and
look at the corresponding hue in the rainbow itself: "Red for the
brilliance of our attraction." (Touch something red.) "Orange for
the joy of our laughter and company together." (Touch an
orange object.) "Yellow for the intellect, marriage of our minds."
(Touch anything yellow.) "Green for the healing we give to each
other." (Touch a green item.) "Blue for the loyalty we willingly
bestow." (Blue object.) "Indigo for the exotic we spark in each
other." (Something indigo blue.) "Violet for the power of our
passion." (Now touch any purple-violet coloured object.)

Now say: "So are we a rainbow of light. Different colours of
our personalities, blended to beauty. May our differences always
make harmony. Rainbow blessings on our love."

A strong love will enter a luckier phase if the words have been
spoken strongly. A weak love will improve its chances of
survival. And an uncommitted love will become more serious.

SALT

A powerful spell-maker, salt has a particular use
for lovers who have had a recent quarrel.

Take some crystal salt flakes and burn them in a candle flame,
or on a fire.

Say out loud the name of the one you love, and repeat the
words: "Salt, salt, I place thee in fire, And may he (or she)
who has bewitched me, make me now his/her heart's desire."

Look into the flames for the face of your love, and send a
powerful message of love through the salty ether.

When you next see your lover, put a flake of salt from the same
source on his tongue very playfully: the bond will now be tied,
and all previous tears, dried.

KEYS

If you find a key on your way to see your loved one, or on your way to meeting someone, the relationship shall grow apace. Do the following:

Place the key in a pocket close to your heart, and wish for fulfillment in love. Wish that your heart may now be fully unlocked, and that love may flow from you to one worthy, someone who may put away any fears you have had of insecurity or unreturned affection.

Take it out again, and hold the key up to the sunshine so that a shaft of light pierces the hole cut in the key. Ask that light may pierce your love life and bring rays of warmth.

Take the key to the house of your love, and put it in some quiet, dark place: a corner, or a drawer, or into a pot. Ask that the light and warmth of your affection spread into your lover's heart, and unlock his or her feelings.

Soon the relationship will unfold with more clarity and security.

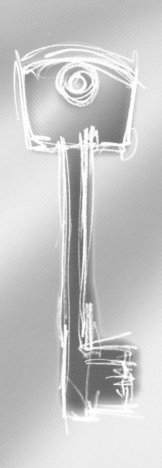

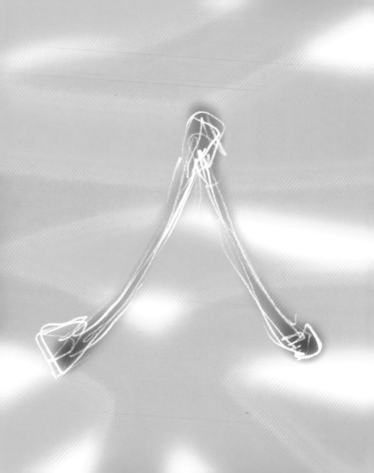

Wishbone

We all know what to do with a wishbone when it falls to us; but if your wish concerns love specifically:

If you get the wishbone, also called the 'merry-thought', place it upon your nose in the manner of spectacles, and close your eyes thinking of your sweetheart. Let it shake off, and then split the bone with another.

If you get the biggest piece, your wish is well on the way to coming true, and your love being everything you hope for, but it should be bound with blue or pink ribbon and put away for safekeeping. The shorter piece, too, you should request back from the other person, and it should be given to your love.

FEATHERS

Symbolic of angel flights, these wonderful talismans can produce very good luck for love.

If you find a white feather, take it up and say your own name as you do, then the name of someone you like, if there is one, or simply say: "Love's token", if there is no one special in your life at the moment.

If you have someone in your heart, place the feather next to a photo of him or her, and promise to give love "light as a feather, soft as silk, uplifting as a cloud". Take these words seriously: a feather used in a spell really demands that you are not too heavy with someone you care for, and that you are reasonable in your handling and expectation of the other person.

If you have no-one in your heart, place the feather against a photo of you, and speak to the angels about your need for someone to enter your life and lighten your heart. Pledge not to make heavy demands on them.

Results could be swift and deeply satisfying.

PRIMROSES AND VIOLETS

The first of either in Spring is an opportunity begging to secure good luck in love:-

When you see the first violet or primrose growing, pluck it and look for the early spring sunshine through your lashes, almost closed.

Take home the flower and place it in a book concerned with love (such as love poems); next to the flower place a picture of your loved one or, if you have no picture, write his or her name on pretty paper. If you love no-one special, put your own picture next to the flower.

Close the book again and light an unused candle beside it; make a powerful wish for love. Before bed, blow out the candle and sleep upon the book.

Luck in love will find you out, wherever you are, before the Spring is over.

Wishing gate or stile

Used extensively in spells and wishes for luck and for love. You will need to make a trip to the countryside, or remember to do this when you are on holiday and the chance arises.

As you go through a gate that opens one way until you pause, and then another as you go out again, kiss your love if he or she is with you, and wish for maximum blessings in your relationship. If you are alone, kiss the palms of both your hands and ask that the love you bear another be returned, or that a new love enter by the gate in your life.

If you are crossing over a stile with two planks of wood set in opposite directions, the spell will be similar to that above: close your eyes and make a wish as you go over it, concerning the hopes you have for one person, or the wish you have of meeting someone. Kiss both your palms.

If you go back by the same gate or stile, do not repeat the wish, for it will undo some of the magic. Your luck in love will change for the better after this.

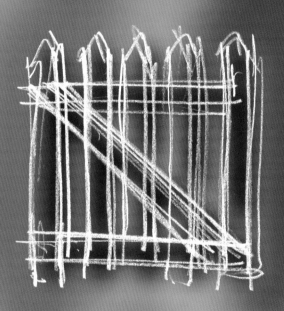

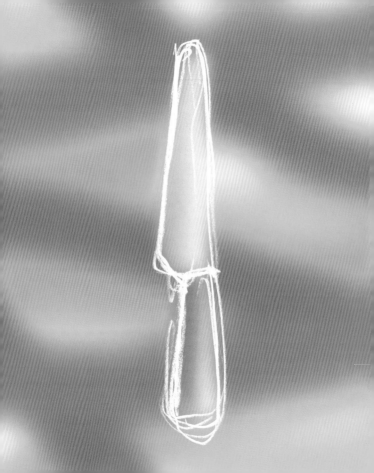

SILVER KNIFE

A prognosticator of the arrival of a man.
If you are male and doing this spell, a fork
should be substituted.

When you drop a silver knife you should make a wish secretly
concerning your love before you pick it up again.

Now tie a blue bow around the handle if you have someone in
your life you wish to be with, or a pink bow if you have not yet
found a true love.

Place the knife in a linen napkin, still be-ribboned,
until your wish is granted.

MOON

When you have just parted from a lover and are feeling down-hearted, the moon will smile kindly on your love life if she is asked properly.

Wait for the new moon, and on the first night go out of doors and hold up a ring near your eye until the moon appears in its circle.

Say: "New Moon, True moon, I hail to thee; In your body milky white, May I see this very night, the man (or woman) who will my partner be."

Now you may see an apparition or a face in the moon; or if a cloud scuds across the moon, your love will be on the way. But in any case, walk backwards from the moon with your eye still on it seen through the ring.

Sleep that night upon the ring, and wear it from now for the next month. During that time you will find at least one new suitor.

HOLLY

A holly bush growing in a garden is said to indicate the dominant partner in a marriage: a male or female bush, accordingly. Holly is also helpful in spells, if you should be given a sprig.

Put a holly leaf over the photo of someone you love.

Saying his or her name, ask that the prickly holly touch you (let it prick your finger) and your lover's heart.

Suck your finger, and kiss your beloved in the picture.

The love will now intensify.

SNAILS

Wonderful creatures which remind us to be patient
in our workings, snails are good friends to lovers.

In any Spring month, if you find a snail, take the little creature
and ask for his help. Place some flour or talc under a rosemary
bush, and put the snail on top of it. Watch for the trail he has
made the following day: the initial of your love will be traced
in the white substance.

Place an ornamental snail over the photo of your heart's desire:
gradually he or she will come to you.

If you have a fireplace, bring a snail in once the ashes of the
previous night's fire have cooled. The snail will, as above,
trace out your truelove's first initial. Let the creature afterwards
go free, showing that your love, too, will always grant your
sweetheart freedom to come and go, and time to him (or her) self.

STOCKINGS

One for girls only – use only a very pretty stocking for this.

If you have not heard from your lover for a few days, or if you have quarrelled a little, pin your stocking on the wall near or above your bed.

Say: "I pin my stocking upon the wall, Hoping my true love will call; Wherever he may presently be, May he not yet happy be, Until he finds or speaks with me."

Concentrate on your love's face, and imagine the stocking stroked by his hands.

Your love will soon contact you, and you must be sweet and not arrogant: never wear that stocking again, but treasure it for luck in love.

DOVES

These are lucky birds for lovers, and portend peace and tranquillity between two people. If you see a dove and need a little luck in love, try this spell:

Look at the dove and blow the creature a kiss with both hands to your mouth simultaneously. Touch your heart and try to feel the gentle beatings like those of the dove's wings.

As quickly after as you are able, write your name entwined with that of the one you love. Take it back to where you saw the dove, and place the entwined names in the fork of a tree.

Lastly, light a white candle and think of the bird in the flame, as well as you and your loved one. Let the candle burn for one hour.

From the next day a new peace will enter your loved one's heart in relation to you.

STAR

When you have just met someone you really like, or have just been with your lover:

Look for a group of stars with which you can just trace out the first letter of your love's first name. Immediately say: "My wishes now are in the stars, May you please guide this love of ours."

Write your lover's name out in full using little star shapes to make up the capital letters.

The next day take them to the sea, or a river or stream, and let them float away, saying: "My love I freely give to thee, May you as freely come to me".

If this love is the one for you, you will steadily be given signs of proof that this is to be, from this day onwards.

THE WOODEN DISH

If marriage is your goal, and you are game,
try this wishing spell:-

On St Swithin's (July 15) or St Valentine's Day, take a wooden
dish outside and place it somewhere it will not be disturbed.
Into the dish you should place a strand of your own hair with
one from your loved one, or if you cannot get this, your initials
scratched together on a leaf.

The next day you must look at the water which has gathered
within the dish. If the water is clean and clear, your lover
will love you, and you alone, more truly than he or she has
ever loved anyone. If it is dirty, or has some blades of grass
in it, you have still some way to go to deepen the love, for
someone else has been in his or her heart and has not yet
completely lost sway. However, the love will now deepen
slowly if you are patient. But if the dish is empty, a relationship
offering you security will not yet be formed, or not with the
one you hope for.

Toss the water from the dish, but keep the names or hair,
and fill the bowl with petals to sweeten the love.

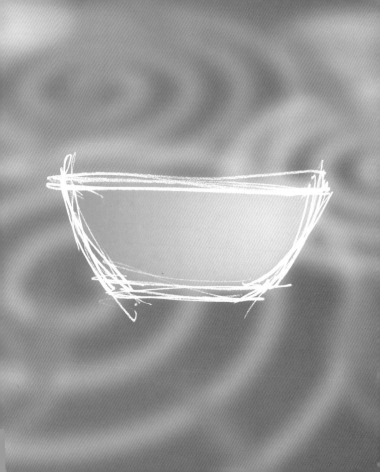

HEARTS

Along the lines that 'like begets like', which is
a powerful premise in magic, this little spell
is designed to make your heart 'grow':

If you are given a little metal or ornamental heart by a friend
(not too precious), you can make your love life flourish by
planting it with love.

Either in your garden, or in a window box, or in a pretty pot,
place the heart with your name written on paper and twined
around it into some earth, and plant a pink flower above it.
Geraniums, roses, daisies, pink hydrangeas or orchids are all
powerful love plants and would do admirably.

Tend the plant carefully: as it blossoms, so will a love affair
blossom for you.

NB: The heart must be given, so you might try asking a
friend for one as a present.

First published in 1999 by Quadrille Publishing Limited,
Alhambra House, 27–31 Charing Cross Road, London WC2H 0LS

PUBLISHING DIRECTOR Anne Furniss

DESIGN Johnson Banks

PRODUCTION Vincent Smith, Julie Hadingham

© TEXT Titania Hardie 1999
© LAYOUT AND DESIGN Quadrille Publishing Ltd 1999

BRITISH LIBRARY CATALOGUING IN PUBLICATION DATA
A catalogue record for this book is available from the British Library

ISBN 1 902757 08 4

PRINTED IN HONG KONG